sheep　　　　trees　　　　meandering roads　　　　bales of hay

apple picking　　　　Memorial Day parades　　　　daisies

fields of wheat　　　　fallen leaves　　　　mill races

farm stands　　　　fishing　　　　cozy old villages　　　　big old oaks

church picnics　　　　geese crossing　　　　ducks migrating

shimmering ponds　　　　lilacs　　　　town auctions on the lawn

old gates　　　　pumpkins　　　　hay rides　　　　daffodils

# Rural Harding

## Fleeting Glimpses

photography by

Jane Austin Kendall

*Jane Austin Kendall*

'Olili Productions

For Rowena MacPhail, an artist and friend, who has always inspired me to see things in new ways, and who has been my partner in so much of this project.

And for David Dietz, my husband, who has been my partner on many life journeys, with more to come.

# foreword

Nature has given this township many gifts, and our predecessors helped to shape and preserve its beauty. We can see evidence of their lives everywhere. Points from Lenape arrows or spears thousands of years old were found by early farmers along Millbrook Road, below Pleasantville Road in the Great Swamp, and many other places. Many of the roads we travel were laid out before the American Revolution, and some of these likely followed old Indian paths. Some of the ditches in the Swamp, especially below Green Village, were created and maintained by farmers of the late 18th and 19th centuries to drain fields where they raised crops. Crumbling stone walls could mark the edges of a field. The remains of some who lived on early farms lie in unmarked graves in tiny cemeteries now lost to all but history.

These remnants speak of hard times and determination in the face of poverty. In the beginning, farming provided a relatively good living, but that time soon ended. Despite hardships, our forefathers made contributions to build and sustain churches and schools before the state provided any funds for schooling. As they still do today, people came together to have fun, often raising money for some good cause at the same time.

This pleasant country has always been a place of refuge from the pressures of the busy marketplace. Peter Kemble, a member of King George III's council that governed the colony of New Jersey, may have been the first to take advantage of this appealing community. After the Revolution, George Logan of Philadelphia tried scientific farming on his lands bordering the Great Swamp. The New York City mason and lighthouse builder John McComb retired to farm near Silver Lake. Throughout the nineteenth century the trend continued: Lord Stirling's great-granddaughter Frances Duer Hoyt and her husband bought the Kemble house and built a new Mount Kemble (later Glen Alpin). Marcellus Hartley Dodge and his bride Geraldine Rockefeller came to the former fresh-air farm of Hartley House looking over Spring Valley, and later Mr. Dodge provided crucial help to preserve the Great Swamp and prevent the placement of a major airport here.

The tree-shaded roads of Harding hide special private places: ravines, the banks of rushing brooks, and high vantage points where a view over wide terrain frees the spirit. In this book, Jane Kendall has captured the ephemeral beauty of nature as the light and seasons change and has caught the innocent expressions of hungry wildlife. She has revealed the character of ancient houses and lovely scenes along our narrow roads. Her book makes clear why so many have worked to ensure that our descendants can also enjoy this bounty.

Mary Prendergast
July 30, 2010

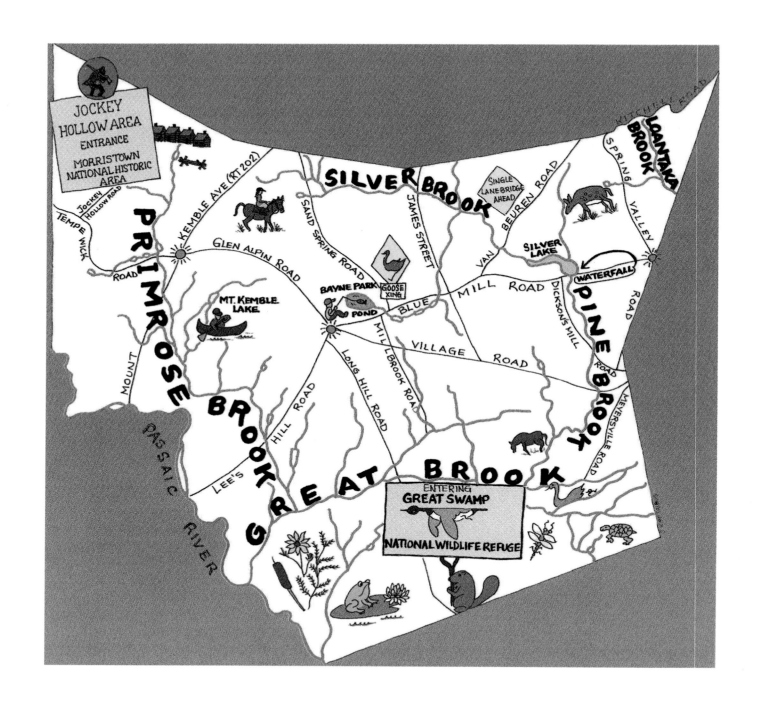

# preface

When I decided to commit my collection of images of Harding to a book, I was already sure I wanted to make a contribution to the town--celebrating its rural and historic legacy.

In looking at my photos for the first time, my friend Wendy Montgomery reminded me that what is significant is not the beauty of the images but the fact that I had taken the vast majority by simply standing along the road...with very few forays into little-known areas of the community.

Harding, like so many old rural towns, proudly reveals itself through its centuries-old streetscapes. Around every bend in the road is another historic home, or stunning vista, or babbling brook, or rustic barn, or quaint stone bridge. Or all of the above next to one another.

The Warren Kinney Memorial Oak Tree has become an icon of what it will take to keep Harding both rural and historically intact. The tree is over 325 years old. Just imagine what it has witnessed in its lifetime. The beautiful old oak gets tender loving care each year. Professional arborists who maintain it are sensitive and honored to be nurturing a tree with such a history. Although the Kinney Oak has major structural supports to keep it from suffering under the weight of its heavy limbs, very thoughtful "surgery" has been done to keep its character intact. And deed restrictions prevent a building being built within a radius of 75 feet. Its survival is a reminder that we have the opportunity to do the same with lands and structures all around us.

Harding is a remarkably compact rural community. Of its 20 square miles, a portion of Great Swamp National Wildlife Refuge occupies six, and Morristown National Historic Park and Loantaka Brook Reservation also contribute to our vast tracks of undeveloped land. Within the remaining acreage are six historic districts, each with a history and culture of its own. Some were home to wealthy gentlemen farmers; others were built as neat little homes for their workers. One in four homes is within one of these districts. Three of our historic districts are on the National and New Jersey State Register of Historic Places. Remnants of old mills and millraces are sprinkled along the meandering streams, which gave life and sustenance to all.

I have pondered how Harding has been able to maintain this rural identity. One key is the passionate commitment of residents to protect this unique community. This book celebrates the buildings and lands that have been preserved with the support of many partners at the local, county, and state level. We are so fortunate to have them available to enjoy today.

So come explore Harding and travel through the timeless sense one has when one meanders down our country lanes.

# acknowledgements

Several people have played important roles in helping me create this book. Each has helped me evolve in my level of clarity about this material, gently encouraging me to become more and more focused.

My dear friend Rowena MacPhail, an accomplished artist and photographer, to whom this book is dedicated, has been my partner throughout this project. Her belief in me, and my body of work, means so much to me. I am forever grateful. Wendy Montgomery has played many roles in relation to my photography and this book. The most important, however, has been in her role as head of Historic Preservation for Harding Township. She has taught to me to see and appreciate our streetscapes and historic heritage. Generosity of spirit, time, knowledge, and creative energy are words that describe my friend Chris Allyn. His knowledge of the history of Harding, our geography, and our historic districts has been invaluable. He also created the informative annotated map, which locates each of the homes and properties in this book--no small task! John Murray, as a friend and as President of Harding Land Trust, has taught me about our land preservation projects, and has been most generous with his time and ideas. Mary Prendergast has astounded me with her level of knowledge about every historic property in Harding. I have appreciated her wise counsel. Tina Bologna, the Executive Director of Harding Land Trust, deserves special thanks for providing me resources along the way. Justine Kovacs has also been helpful from the moment I really committed to this book. Thanks, also, to Bernice Paton, Bill Paton, Joan Baumgarten as well as Jim Bellis and Gus Koven. Many others have given of their time and energy along the way. Each has helped me grow in my ability to present the best of Harding. I thank them all.

Gordon Thomas Ward is a gifted poet and writer. I am so touched by his poem, Acre, and so appreciative of his willingness to include it in this book.

We all owe a huge debt of gratitude to the women and men throughout our community's history who have had the foresight, the will, and the fortitude to work so hard to save what makes Harding so special in its historic and rural character. From those who worked to preserve our land and homes to those who successfully fought off the construction of Port Authority's fourth jetport, where Great Swamp National Wildlife Refuge now stands; they have all understood how precious our heritage is.

Odette Rickert, my book designer, editor, and publisher has taught me so much about the world of publishing and has patiently helped structure the project to reach fruition, and all of this long distance, with Odette living in Hawaii.

Lastly, I am blessed to have an amazing life partner and husband, David Dietz, who has played many roles throughout the years I have been photographing Harding: creative partner, critic, educator, advisor. His knowledge of Harding, the master plan, easements, and other diverse subjects has added yet another perspective to my work.

*spring*

"*Kids used to walk through the woods to each other's homes--without ever walking on a road.*"

Rowena MacPhail

"Most years around fourth of July, our friends have a "Natural Fireworks Party". We gather at their home. Over the years at about 9PM, armed with flashlights, we go down to Dickson's Mill Road (the Koven Property preserved in 1990) and stand in just about the middle of the property on the road down past the bridges and we watch. The lights that appear from the lightening bugs are the most amazing thing! It looks like white Christmas lights everywhere! They even seem to blink in succession! Those are "the natural fireworks."  It is truly a wondrous thing. It would not be possible without the preservation of that large piece of land and most importantly, no street lights, house lights, etc. It is a great event and makes us all appreciate where we live."

Jane Riley

"There was Mill Pond, where the stream on Dickson's Mill Road now is. The mill was on the left side. Across the road, the white bank house set up from the road is where my parents lived. The mill was taken down, and then they took down the stone walls. The pond became a stream. My mother didn't want the land to be built up, as she heard some developers talking about, so she bought it, and eventually it became the first donation to the Harding Land Trust."

Ted Koven

"*I am sure that the original settlers of Harding would be pleasantly surprised to see the Township as it exists today. A decision by some of the larger landowners in 1928 to place restrictive covenants on their land and break from the Passaic County Charter probably got a glancing mention in the evening newspaper. Today, we know it was the tipping point that sets Harding apart from all other communities in Morris County. A town built on its agricultural and rural heritage with a social and historic fabric so strong it binds this extraordinary community together like no other. It is now up to the next generation to make sure that the values of our founders are preserved in perpetuity. We are the stewards of these large open vistas, hedgerows, fields, and dense forests. We have a moral obligation to leave a small footprint and dark skies.*"

Nicolas W. Platt

### POLO FIELDS

THE SITE OF THE WORLD'S LARGEST ONE DAY DOG
SHOW 1927 - 1957, THE MORRIS & ESSEX KENNEL
CLUB HOSTED BY GERALDINE ROCKEFELLER
DODGE THE POLO FIELD HAS BEEN PLACED ON THE
NATIONAL & STATE REGISTERS OF HISTORIC PLACES.

IN A UNIQUE PARTNERSHIP BETWEEN THE NEW
JERSEY AUDUBON SOCIETY AND HARTLEY FARMS,
THIS FIELD HAS BEEN PROTECTED FROM FUTURE
DEVELOPMENT IN PERPETUITY AND IS NOW A
PERMANENT SANTUARY FOR WILDLIFE.

NEW JERSEY
AUDUBON
SOCIETY

NATIONAL HISTORIC LANDMARK

"As I drive along Van Beuren, I enjoy seeing all the markings of a rural town: old farms, cattle grazing along the fence, and a brook meandering under our one lane bridge."

Larry Prendergast

*summer*

*"My childhood in the early 1950s meant riding my shiny red tricycle on Lee's Hill Road with no supervision as hardly a car went by and those that did were friends or neighbors. Lee's Hill was unpaved--a gravel road--until 1956."*

Meredith (Dithy) Schroeder Limmer

*"Though my parents' home, at the major intersections of Lee's Hill, Village, Blue Mill, and Glen Alpin is a landmark property, beloved by many residents and non-residents alike, will it be restored, renovated properly, or destroyed?"*

Meredith (Dithy) Schroeder Limmer

"I never realized how much sound, natural and manmade, weaves through the fabric of a community. The bell of the Methodist Church in Green Village rang in our Sunday mornings for decades."

Penny Hinkle

HARDING LAND TRUST

# WATERMAN MEADOW

· · ·

This 19 acre meadow was permanently preserved in 2001 through the generosity of the family of Robert and Elizabeth Waterman in partnership with the Harding Land Trust, the Township of Harding, the Morris County Open Space Preservation Trust and the State of New Jersey Green Acres Program.

The land was part of the estate of Marcellus Hartley Dodge until the Watermans acquired it in 1951. The Pump House, built in 1907, was restored by the Harding Land Trust as an example of outbuilding architecture from the era.

MARGETTS FIELD

DEDICATED TO THE MEMORY OF
WALTER T. MARGETTS AND JOSEPHINE S. MARGETTS,
DISTINGUISHED CITIZENS OF HARDING TOWNSHIP
WHO LOVED THIS FIELD, THIS COMMUNITY
AND OUR COUNTRY ENVIRONMENT.

ACQUIRED BY HARDING TOWNSHIP IN 1992
WITH THE ASSISTANCE OF THE MARGETTS FAMILY
WITHOUT WHOSE GOOD WILL, PATIENCE
AND SUPPORT THIS LOVELY FIELD COULD NOT
HAVE BEEN PRESERVED.

"*The combination of hills, vistas, white painted gates, woodlands, stream corridors, stone bridges and historic properties is like none other! Every winding road is a masterpiece for us to enjoy.*"

Justine Kovacs

*"When we moved here, there were 84 miles of bridle trails. People built homes along the bridle trails."*

Bernice Paton

*If its many volunteers are the heart of Harding, its rural vistas, both farmland and open space, are its soul. The whole character of what we value most about Harding centers on its inspiring farms and fields and soothing wooded area. Take away a significant portion of the nearly 50% of Harding that is preserved and we would be living in a different place entirely.*

John Murray

"As responsible citizens, we don't own
our land, we are stewards of our land.
We hope to pass it on in better shape
than we received it."

Edgar Anderson

"We are fortunate to live and drive by the landscapes you have captured. They are owned by residents who take pride in their properties and want to share them visually with others. Open fields, meadows, streams, colonial houses, historic barns and 100 year old oaks capture the eye and provide us with beauty that calms our souls. The scenes humble us to recall that there is a God."

Jay Kemmerer

"I enjoy the feeling when we have been away and we get off the highway at Route 202 and make the turn onto Bailey's Mill Road and we go over the bridge and I feel like I am on vacation all over again. The greenery, the gentle stream, the hills, the deer (love/hate), the birds, etc. The absolute tranquility."

Jane Riley

# Acre

An acre of land to breathe upon
Surrounded by historic woods,
What stories are told in the whispering trees
As they sway
Back and forth,
Boreal metronomes
Animated by the wind?
Come hither and listen.
Our stories are many
Of long withered lives
And times long forgotten.

An acre of land alone in time,
How many feet have trod your soil?
The Lenape held sacred this ground,
Their mother, provider of provisions and shelter.
Her fibers contained the spirits of forefathers.
Many farmers followed with plows
To cut the brown, productive earth,
Preparing to sow.
Their cattle have grazed
Past barbed, pasture wire,
Now swallowed by the trees and time,
So that the neglected, rusted metal
Now appears to grow
From the middle
Of the rough, expanding trunks
Like cinnamon whiskers.
The brook speaks in sparkling echoes
Of all the explorers who searched its banks
In rolled-up overalls
Searching for crayfish beneath the stones,
Abandoning boots their mothers had sent.

An acre of land to celebrate
The joys of life,
How many holidays have you seen?
Groves of Christmas trees must have graced
This unassuming residence
With carols, turkey, and pumpkin pie
And angels bending near.
The lawn embraced the family groups
Who gathered for games
On the Fourth of July
While fathers cooked dinners on open flames.
I fancied aromas still carried on the breeze.
I can almost hear the laughter of children
Who played in the yard
Until day turned to dusk,
And they were called to wash and bed,
Leaving the yard
To fireflies and wild nightsounds.
Innumerable pumpkins
Illuminated the porch,
Hollowed in haste
And carved with demonic faces,
Designed to dispel demons
And tempt ghostly figures
Carrying candy sacks
Under their shrouds.

An acre of land to call my own,
To manage as I please,
What evidence does it hold
Of previous proprietors
Who expressed their love and respect for the land
Through labor and sweat?
They, who once touched the stones upon which I
walk,
Now claim eternal marking stones
In churchyards down the country road,
Which I touch in respectful remembrance.
We have sought the shade of the same trees
And taken shelter in this house
Through thunder and ice.
We have survived
All that nature has offered us,
Given all that we could give,
Endured our private trials and joys.

An acre of land
Is more than a measured lot of earth.

An acre of land upon my hands…
What will my signature be?

Gordon Thomas Ward
© 2007

*autumn*

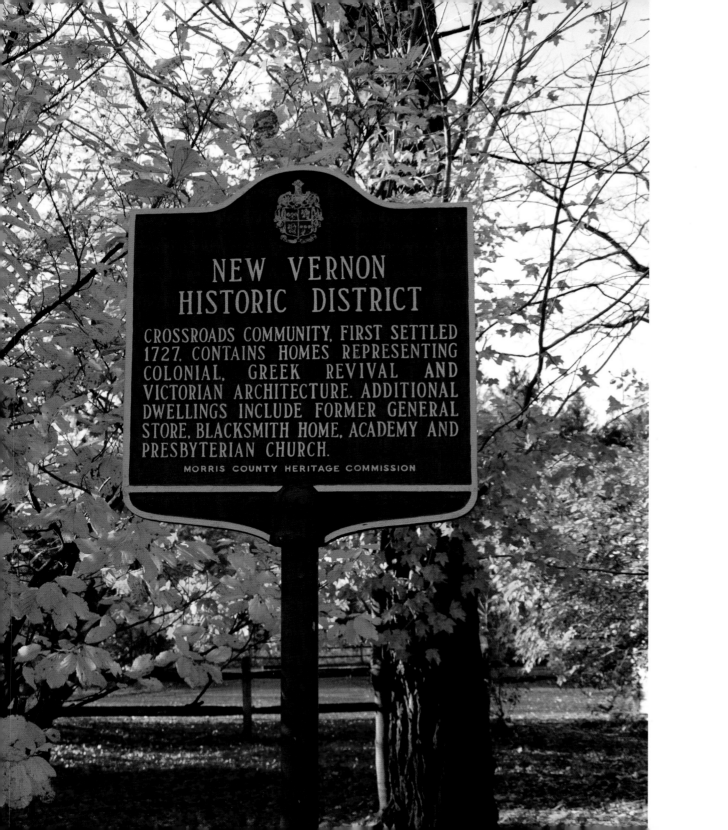

NEW VERNON
HISTORIC DISTRICT

CROSSROADS COMMUNITY, FIRST SETTLED
1727, CONTAINS HOMES REPRESENTING
COLONIAL, GREEK REVIVAL AND
VICTORIAN ARCHITECTURE. ADDITIONAL
DWELLINGS INCLUDE FORMER GENERAL
STORE, BLACKSMITH HOME, ACADEMY AND
PRESBYTERIAN CHURCH.

MORRIS COUNTY HERITAGE COMMISSION

"Harding's meadows, woods, and brooks are remarkable repositories of fast-vanishing nature. Landscapes, hedgerows, barns, and stone foundations carry traces of human history. Preserved at the heart of Harding, the Great Swamp is the nursery of its natural world."

Penny Hinkle

*"You always knew it was fall by the smell of burning leaves."*

Jim Bellis

*"After working to save township trees for a few years, I learned that the best way to save a tree is to save the land it grows on...for me, and my family, that was the beginning of a very long quest to treasure and save the vistas and woodlands in our beautiful rural Harding."*

Justine Kovacs

*winter*

"When I look back over nearly 50 years of life in Harding, the first thing that comes to mind is the openness and horses. They really go together, most of the land owners had, on average, larger properties and the space to house and graze horses and ponies. If you didn't want the care and maintenance of your horses there were always four or five commercial stables that would care for your horse and if it was a hunt day they would have your horse ready to go. Today these stables are for the most part dedicated to the show horse crowd, not local trail riders.

The residents kept their land open if only the edges of their fields to give the hunt a "way around". The properties were connected by a series of bridle paths and grazing pastures were separated by split rail fences, stone walls, or chicken coops. You had to jump these obstacles to keep up with the hunt. The hunt was a "drag" hunt. A fox scent was dragged around the countryside the morning of the hunt and the pack of 10 to 20 hounds had to follow it. This made for a faster hunt than a live fox hunt and made it easier to keep the hounds (not dogs) packed up.

Not everyone "hunted". There were many horse shows at the show grounds and two or three times a year a hunter pace and hunter trials. These trials were held in an area covering the major part of the open fields that are still visible on either side of Red Gate Road. Festivities included a tea back at the hunt masters home at the end of the trials; all were invited. The hunter pace covered most of the farm portions of the township and could be up to 12 miles. A large portion of the "hunt country" was in the great swamp and (what is now) Loantaka Brook Park area."

Bill Paton

"When I think of rural Harding, I think of driving by the vast open fields, like Margetts and Frelinghuysen, which cover the landscape. We are so fortunate that our community has been able to preserve this oasis that is so close to New York City,"

Tom MacCowatt

"As a result of 80 years of concerted efforts to preserve the landscape of Harding made by generations of dedicated and generous people, Harding Township is as beautiful today as it has been in the past. We, the present generation, have an obligation to continue these efforts, and we will do so."

Marshall Bartlett

# Harding map points and historic districts

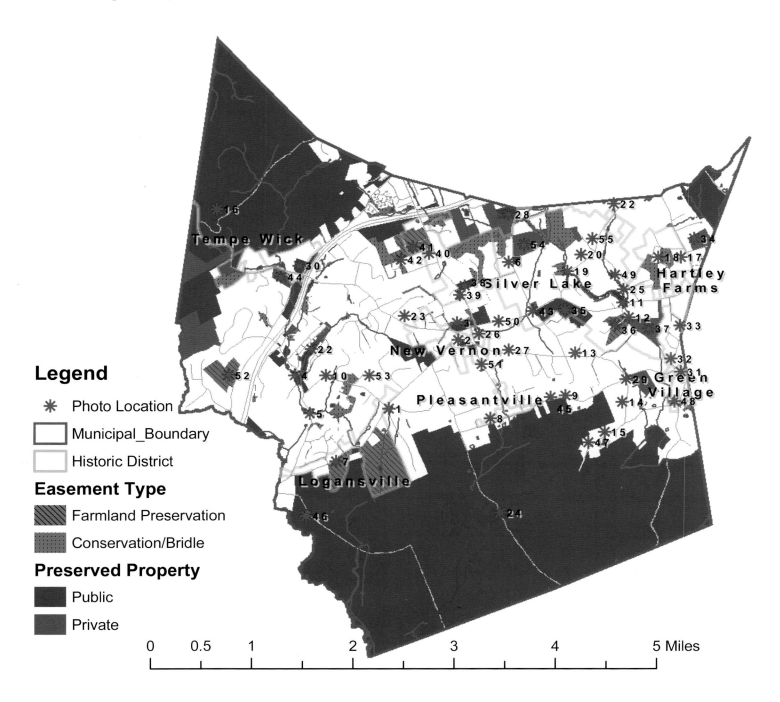

**Legend**

|  | |
|---|---|
| ✳ | Photo Location |
| ☐ | Municipal_Boundary |
| ☐ | Historic District |

**Easement Type**

| | |
|---|---|
| ▨ | Farmland Preservation |
| ▦ | Conservation/Bridle |

**Preserved Property**

| | |
|---|---|
| ■ | Public |
| ■ | Private |

0   0.5   1   2   3   4   5 Miles

# index of photographs

# index of photographs (continued)

# index of photographs (continued)

Note: The names attributed to historic houses are those recognized by the Historic Preservation Commission and listed in the McCabe Survey, dated 2004.

## 'Olili Productions

Hilo, Hawai'i
www.OliliProductions.com

*Rural Harding: Fleeting Glimpses* by Jane Austin Kendall

Jacket design, all photos, and contents
Copyright © 2010 Jane Austin Kendall
ALL RIGHTS RESERVED

www.janekendallphotography.com

First Printing - September 2010
Library of Congress Control Number:  2010910768
ISBN:  978-0-9842543-9-2

NO PART OF THIS BOOK MAY BE REPRODUCED IN ANY FORM, BY PHOTOCOPYING OR ANY OTHER ELECTRONIC
OR MECHANICAL MEANS, INCLUDING INFORMATION STORAGE OR RETRIEVAL SYSTEMS, WITHOUT PERMISSION IN
WRITING FROM THE COPYRIGHT OWNER/AUTHOR.

Thanks to Harding Land Trust for the use permission of the hand drawn map of Harding Township drawn by Janet Tribus, 2000.
Thanks to Gordon Thomas Ward for the use permission of his poem, Acre, copyright © 2007.
Thanks to Chris Allyn for the creation and use permission of his Harding Map Points and Historic Districts map, 2010.

Cover photo:  Pine Brook on Koven donated property
Back cover photo:  Bayne Park
Inside front panel:  Kinney Oak, c. 1685
Inside rear panel:  43 Lake Trail West, Mt. Kemble Lake

Offset printed by Mira Digital Publishing on paper that is FSC, SFI, and PEFC certified

Printed in the United States of America

babbling brook      open fields      farms      horses

wide vistas      open horizons      wooden bridges

firehouse      old churches      horse farms      wood houses

weather vanes      canoes      waterfalls      herons

wooden fence      flowering trees      eating hotdogs

old chimneys      stone walls      horse trails      bike rides

the Swamp in early morning      golden sunsets      deer